WITH

MARBLES

By Eiji Orii and Masako Orii   Pictures by Kaoru Fujishima

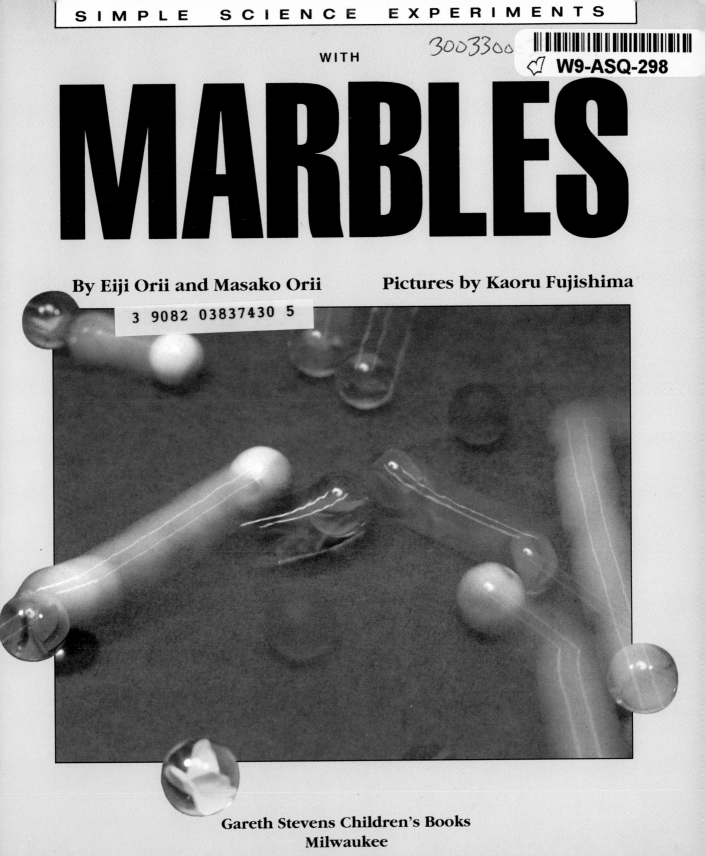

Gareth Stevens Children's Books
Milwaukee

Library of Congress Cataloging-in-Publication Data

Orii, Eiji, 1909-
    Simple science experiments with marbles / Eiji Orii and Masako Orii;
Kaoru Fujishima (ill.). — North American ed.
        p.   cm. — (Simple science experiments)
    Translated from the Japanese.
    Includes index.
    Summary: Presents experiments using marbles to demonstrate what
happens when something which is moving hits something else.
    ISBN 1-555-32856-3 (lib. bdg.)
    1. Force and energy—Experiments—Juvenile literature.
2. Collisions (Physics)—Experiments—Juvenile literature.
[1. Force and energy—Experiments. 2. Collisions (Physics)-
-Experiments. 3. Experiments.] I. Orii, Masako. II. Fujishima,
Kaoru, ill. III. Title. IV. Series.
QC73.4.075   1989
531'.3—dc19   88-23297

North American edition first published in 1989 by

Gareth Stevens Children's Books
7317 West Green Tree Road
Milwaukee, Wisconsin 53223, USA

This US edition copyright ©1989. First published as B*idama Wa Kazu Wo Shitteiru (Let's Try Glass Marbles)* in
Japan with an original copyright © 1986 by Eiji Orii, Masako Orii, and Nittosha Co., Ltd. English translation
rights arranged with Dainippon-Tosho Publishing Co., Ltd., through Japan Foreign-Rights Centre, Tokyo.

Additional text and illustrations copyright © 1989 by Gareth Stevens, Inc.

Series editor and additional text: Rita Reitci
Research editor: Scott Enk
Additional illustrations: John Stroh
Design: Laurie Shock
Translated from the Japanese by Jun Amano
Technical consultant: Jonathan Knopp, Chair, Science Department, Rufus King High School, Milwaukee

2 3 4 5 6 7 8 9 94 93 92 91 90 89

What do a rolling marble and a rocket ship drifting in space
have in common? Both have momentum, the force of a
moving object.

Momentum must always go somewhere, unless stopped by
another force. It cannot go alone; it needs something to
travel in. It can jump into another object or be shared among
several. It can change direction and it can even bounce back.

By using marbles and coins, you can find out more about
what momentum does when different combinations of
moving objects meet objects that are at rest.

Use two rulers or straight pieces of wood to make a track for some marbles. Tape the rulers about half an inch (1 cm) apart side by side on a table or a smooth floor. Be sure the table or floor is level so that the marbles do not roll by themselves. If you can, use marbles of the same colors as those shown in this book.

Place two marbles of the same size inside the track. Flick the yellow marble at the green marble. What happens?

The green marble stops the yellow one. But the moving force, or momentum, of the yellow marble enters the green one, making it roll.

What happens if you hold the green marble and hit it with the yellow one?

The green marble cannot move. So the moving force, or momentum, pushes the yellow marble back.

Put one marble in the track next to another one of the same size so that they touch. Now put a third marble in the track and shoot it at these two. What happens this time?

The blue marble stops. Its moving force, or momentum, travels through the yellow marble and into the pink one. The pink marble rolls.

The momentum of the blue marble is just enough to move one marble of its own size and weight.

What happens when you hold the yellow marble and strike it with another?

The pink one rolls. The momentum of the blue marble travels through the yellow one, and into the pink marble.

9

What happens when you hold the pink marble and strike the yellow one with the blue one?

The blue one bounces back. What is pushing the blue marble? Where does the momentum travel?

Put three marbles, all the same size, in your track so that they touch. Shoot at the yellow marble with the red marble. What happens?

The purple one rolls. This time, does the moving force, or momentum, from the red marble go into the purple one? What path does the force travel to get there? Is the momentum enough to move three marbles? Two marbles?

Hold the yellow marble and flick the red marble at it. Again, the purple one rolls.

You should now be able to tell what will happen when you hold the blue marble and strike the yellow one with the red one.

Tell where the momentum will travel when you hold the purple marble and strike the yellow one with the red one.

Put three coins on a table with a smooth top. Coins A and B are touching. You want to get coin C between them. First make a space between coins A and B without touching either coin A or coin B with your hands. How can you do this?

Hint: Look on page 8 at the experiment with marbles to see how you can make the space you need. Now you can slide coin C into the space between coin A and coin B without touching either.

Place three marbles in the track, all touching one another.
Use two marbles touching each other as shooters. Flick the
red marble. What happens?

Now the momentum of two rolling marbles travels into the resting marbles. The force is strong enough to make two marbles roll, the yellow and green ones.

What happens when you hold the blue marble and flick the red one?

The yellow and green marbles roll.

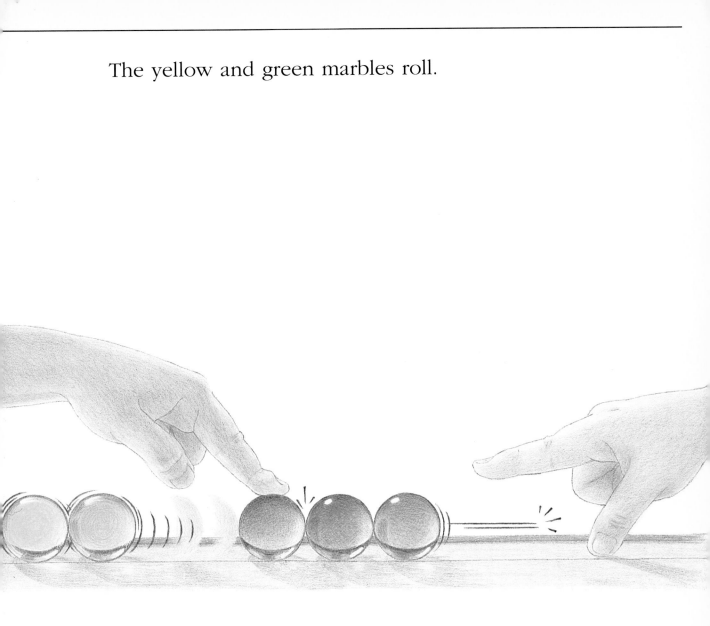

But what happens when you hold the green one?
What if you hold the yellow one?

Try this experiment with lots of marbles and see what happens. Find out where the momentum travels and how many marbles it will move.

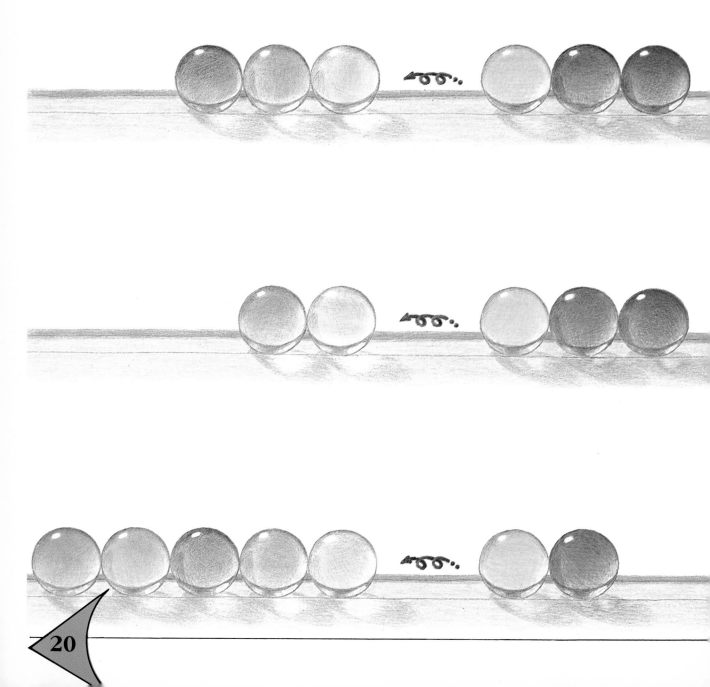

Swinging balls show how momentum travels.

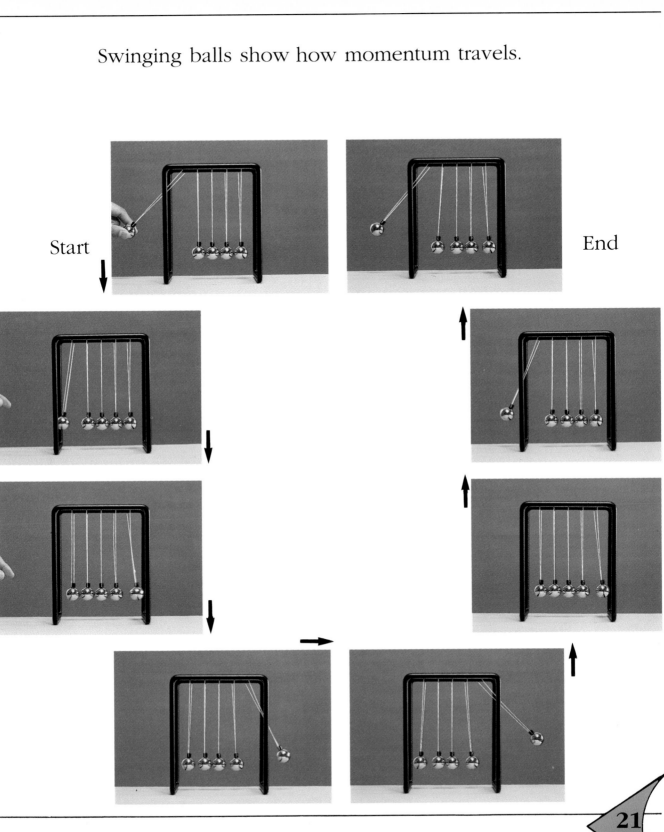

Start

End

Try marbles of different sizes. What will happen when you shoot a small marble at a large one?

The small marble bounces away from the large one. But some of its momentum enters the large marble and moves it.

The amount of momentum stays the same. But it is now shared by the two marbles.

Find out what happens when you hit the small marble with the large one.

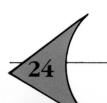

Both marbles roll in the same direction. How fast are they going?

Heavy moving objects have more momentum than lighter ones going the same speed. Enough momentum goes from the large marble into the small one to move it.

The remaining momentum keeps the large marble rolling.

Keep adding small marbles. Strike them with a large marble.

Find out if there is enough momentum to move all of the marbles you add.

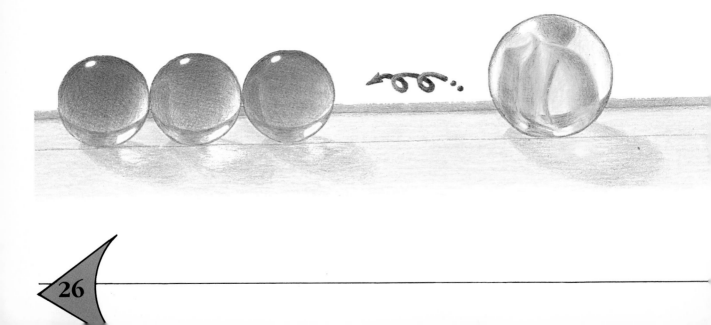

Put three coins in a row on a smooth tabletop so that they touch. What happens when you flick a fourth coin so it hits coin C?

Try this with other coins.

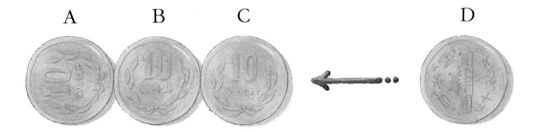

Coin A moves. The momentum from coin D travels through coins C and B to move coin A.

A   B   C   D

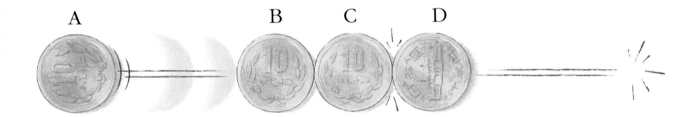

Place five coins in the positions you see here. Be sure all the coins touch. Now hit coin D with coin F.

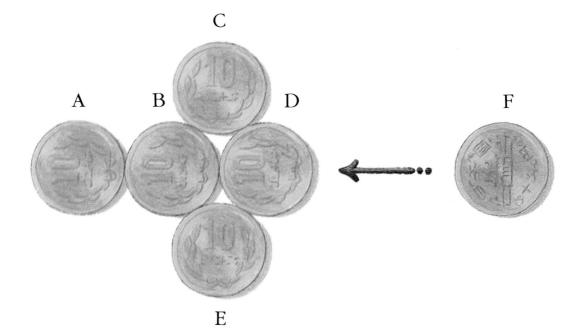

Again, coin A moves. The momentum from coin F moves in a straight line through coins D and B and into coin A.

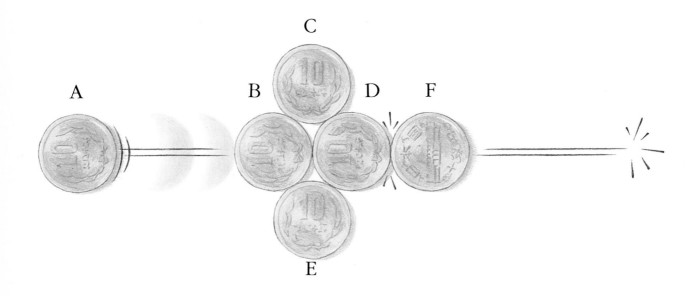

This time move coins A and B away from the other coins. Now strike coin D with coin F. What happens? Remember that momentum can be shared.

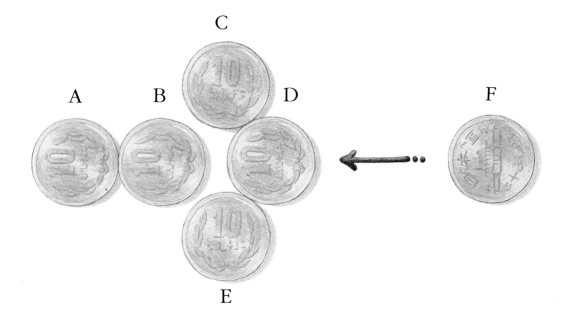

Look at the small drawing on top of p. 32 for the answer. By now, you should not be surprised by all the things momentum can do!

GLOSSARY

Here is a list of words used in this book. After you read what each word means, you can see it used in a sentence.

experiment: a test or trial to find out about something
Her experiment taught her about things she did not know about moving and resting objects.

flick: to flip, to lightly hit, to touch
He flicked dust from his suit.

force: a power, a strength, an influence
The wind is so powerful a force that it can turn heavy windmills.

marbles: little balls of stone, clay, or glass, used in games that are also known as marbles. At one time these balls were made of real marble, and the streaked pattern of some modern marbles resembles this stone. The game of marbles began in ancient times, and is played today in many lands. Marble championship matches are held in various parts of the United States, and there is also a yearly national tournament.
He lost a lot of marbles in yesterday's games.

momentum: the moving force of an object in motion
The momentum of her swing carried her high into the air.

object: a thing, something that can be seen or touched
There were six objects of different colors, shapes, and sizes on the kitchen table.

remaining: the part of something that is left over
She used the remaining soap for washing dishes.

share: to divide something among two or more objects or persons
The boys will share the kitchen chores today.

shoot: to move with great speed or sudden force; to flick one marble at one or more other marbles
They will shoot the rapids in their canoe.

shooters: the marbles used to strike other marbles
He won the game with his new glass shooter.

track: a set of rails along which something can run
He laid his toy railroad track around the room.

INDEX